catastrophes

Carolynne Garcia

Presentation by *BookLeaf Publishing*

Web: www.bookleafpub.com

E-mail: info@bookleafpub.com

ISBN: 9789357442220

First edition 2023

words

i create these beautiful things in my mind but they quickly escape from it, not wanting to be written on paper. they deserve so much more, so i never get the chance to actually see them in front of me. they're probably afraid like me, afraid that nobody will understand them and treat them the way words should be. they're fragile and misunderstood, but as they grow through me like vines and pass by like death, i will soon see that they were made to be shown like skin and shine like the sky, so effortlessly bright.

hostage rhyme

the eyes are the movement that set things in
motion
the warmth that shelters you from shivering
oceans
fingers caressing walls, shadow playing in
obscurity and all
its the melody you hum during the stale
moments in company halls
it shows like technicolour cartoons prancing in
hearts
that fuse without a spark to ignite
you try to avoid, a dangerous cause
what if i explore like a child, with no flaw
electricity running through my veins
contact charges up the excitement
could my curious purpose awake return
and it's favor burn
a will to seek a muse and be your beloved
a sweeping thought bursting like staining news
my doubt not concerning itself with future
mistakes of what's reeling in your brain
can eyes be deceiving?
i can be naive sometimes but oh
cherry sweet, i can't wait to see

back to december

your nocturnal heart is one i dream
to be near, heavy with the mixture
of desire and pleasure
bring your fingertips to my crown
as you slip me facedown
remember you are the only one who
put me onto hands and knees
pleading with "yes" and "please"
while you hold onto my frame
since day one, you've gained
parts to my weary heart
the car that sometimes hesitates to start
perfect sense to combust
locked eyes with your moonlit lust
you're heavens man made gift
a reminder that i seem to want to forget
i close my observers to try and recreate
the dream i never want to escape

the cycles of connection

I

auburn, yellow, ginger,
like the leaves or the colour of your hair
the beauty, the chaos of it all,
it causes this chemical reaction-
Al and Br collide and we come alive

II

crimson wine, cupid time
dimmed lights, midnight strikes
winter breeze hit our blushed faces
being red was an understatement
i knew i've seen your eyes somewhere
i used to stare at them in the stars,
praying to them to be shown in human form

III

we sit and watch the waves break,
crash collide into unbounded ultramarine
white shadows present my flushed face

feelings felt, but not spoken showed the pace
aged blue combing into sweet cherry
oh darling, how you made lilac sweep into our
hearts

IV

boxes and an unpacking truck
lemon's scent surrounding us
brick or wood walls
it never seemed fast at all
new setting, coaxing us into serenity
we may be far from our meeting place,
but home is being in your company

V

lust sky's, bright eyes
we inhale and oxygen becomes heavy,
entering a state of blissful energy
holding onto each other
merging into one another
is it too soon to be nearing
as i feel your breathing
while we lying awake on a rainy day

VI

midnight city irradiates
fluorescent glow smiling down on us
we gave off our best show
but deep down
we knew we had failed
the love we tried to keep alive
was tearing us apart

VII

we never meant to wake up the neighborhood
our yelling was just a cry out for help
make up or break up, we told ourselves
oblivious to the words we threw like daggers
the pain we caused felt good at first
but we left incurable scars
glass shattered hearts was the conclusion

VIII

despair in the atmosphere
inhaling the reality of this outcome
distinctive parts of you

i'd say you were like river sand, but beach sand
suits you better
concoctions rough
fragments left behind, jumpers and depictions
circling 'round my mind
let adoration live on in the continuity up above
us
the people will soon see it was devotion other
than amusement

dear april,

april, you were supposed to be different
i prayed things would turn out like july
praying you'd love me and take care of me like
july, he did that but i was too blinded to see, too
dumb to invite him in
 i said goodbye to him days later
threw him away like august's falling leaves
knew it was a mistake but oh well
but april, things were supposed to be-
you said you cared, why'd you do it then?
i tested the waters 5 days back in january
guess i was cursed since that one night in
february when i fell head in, deep, so far gone
april, why'd you reel me in all those months
when you could've prevented the falling in and
out of love in cupid's retched world
should i keep going?
how dare you, did you ever feel remorse
i wish the guilt would eat you up like
those sleepless, crying nights did to me
oh well, i was troubled and you understood
familiar in so many ways
found a crack through my skin, oh wait
it's just another map to you
your 5th one right? you said you loved me

oh wait, tell that to your 3rd one every night
reeled her in too for a year it seems
third petal down, real showcasing of a thorn in
flesh
made it very known it was her you were with
valentine's night
but let's not talk about the flowers you've picked
or the ones you shouldn't have picked
im not done yet
the wishing and pleading you would change
oh i was the puppet in your shadow play
had me by my strings, you'd push and pull
you'd say "kiss me" and i'd lay myself down
like horizontal views
dragged me along from late winter to early
spring
so draining, my colors were slowly fading
how could you? kept up the act
will you only feel bad when they find out?that it
was never all real
what was happening between us, your lies
revealed
it still hurts, tears and ideals
it's sad i know i'll heal, but at last
i've cut the visible lines connected to you
took a while but now we're in may
and once again i am in charge.

spring lifeline

all i want is him, just him but the inconsistency, the going back and forth, the lack of feeling loved, although i only ever feel "loved" when you touch my skin and when you kiss the creases of my mouth and stare into the soul of my image, yes that's the only time i ever feel "loved". but when i dont: you're attached to the device that keeps you out of reach, you'll only ever touch my hand here and there just to come back from it, you'll lie on your back and tell me that i'm special but lack the courage and movement to do it and show me, you'll kiss me and say you like me, but i can taste the hesitance to spill the actual truth and i can see right through the faded forced smile and hooded eyes that the actuality is you only feel a small, sort of pity type, of friendly love, the kind that just by getting to know me, i reminded you of her, those 5,6 qualities of familiarity and you latched on, deciding i was the 2nd best closest thing you'd ever get to her. and it stuck in the back of my head like old chewing gum; every single place we'd visit or song listened to, i'd overthink if it reminded you of her. that doubt i always feel linger through on out, it seeped through your

mind and thoughts and poured into mine like
water and oil, heavy and mixed; i guess the
mixture of the pained sadness reached me cause
that's the only constant thing i've felt since i've
met you that one november night.

replacement

say you miss me, minds winding
that you love me, was skeptical
poker face and shield up half way
should've never let you in
didn't know the expiration date called for less
than a month away
should've known i was the stepping stone
into another monthly exhibit
where you forget about the one before me
talk the walk gallery
stranded the next valley
go out looking for your next potential hit
got a fetish, it's dealing amateurish
but the band aids ripped
a slap to the head, almost a miss
has it hit yet? when you mentioned the tag along
girl days after you saw me crying, begging to
your face
guess i mistook you for the take it easy crowd
clearly you're apart of the whoever's next and
around
you'll let anyone in, just to soothe and caress the
wounds you've so clearly never cared to patch
up

this love and hurt presenting itself in its
unflattering ways
weighing a ton to point where my face turns red
and my hands gone blue
where i see you in the distance
cant tell if you're angry or hurt too?

a letter to my parents

i have been taught to love you
but i have not received that love
yea you're mom and dad
but are you what i so desperately desire

i think you think i'm a disappointment
sorry if i am
if i'm not your ideal, perfect daughter
sorry that i may not want to live
the life you choose forced for me
maybe you're better off without me
maybe everyone is

i wish everything would've worked out
why am i so needy
why do i crave to be touched
or even a simple hug
maybe if dad wouldn't have left
or maybe if he actually loved mom

i remember the lullabies you'd sing to me
but i don't remember the kisses you gave me
where are they now, where's the "i love you" or
the "i appreciate what you do"
can you please tell me before it's too late!

i can only cry out for help for so long
before i run out of breathe
i hope you'll see right through the fake smiles
my eyes are getting tired now

can you please tell me you love me before i say
it
seems like every time i do
it patches up what i've pulled

maybe if i go
if i push the button
disappear
poof
now you can restart and rebuild
the child that you really wanted

why do i keep crying?

i cried out for you a couple months back
from what i've lacked
all the tears i shed the last few years
and i'm still crying
some still got the same reasons
others for newly opened wounds

yearning for a warm embrace
the "father" figure i chase
and somehow i sit next to a stranger
my mind seeking high praise
silly girl, look
you beg everything from nothingness
something that i thought was once there
slowly slips like the memories i held onto
i want to hold onto the man
who once took care of me at age six
but now even i can't remember
the last time you gave me a goodbye kiss

i know you've forgotten
to even ask how i've been feeling
don't even think you have the right
yet you correct me any way you can
it stings to not even hold a conversation

wishing my sister were here
she knows how to talk to you
better than i ever could
after all she always knew
and i avoided you
from some reason i just couldn't
talk the way she did

the path not taken

i plead
with innocent eyes of the dying breed
i want to be free
with an iron heart of passion and rid myself of
the greed that tries to slither into my reach
frame of a maturing adolescent
but mind and spirit of the child who's still stuck
trying to learn how to preach
i want to remain this way and never arrive to the
destination that is misery's beach
for i know in my observing line of view
mother never really taught with a clue
as to how i should continue
lessons learned from early blues
it's almost like i've memorized the cue
tough but i know i'll get there soon
with the stones i've placed in front
no rear viewing, eyes up
i steer clear of unwinding personified who's

back to december

it was as easy as saying id never lose you
one two was locked in
loaded with days in advance
i feel this pit in my stomach
and i cant face this torture
of december splashed onto the night
where i'd repaired and restored
what was once mine
you blew fresh, familiar air and i seemed to have
halted in my process
of curing august's access
clear of intention it seemed
you pry and seek like ones before
but this time worse than the others
and it sits and settles like these covers on
my chest and back
suffocating but comforting
yea maybe i lost a few screws on my way
as i lack the tongue to express
and here i thought you were my compass

bittersweet

why do you avoid me?
am i that easy to forget, to dispense?
erase the trial and errors of our suspense
am i not what you wanted
i see you, yes i do
ghosting through the halls
emotional transparency as i recall
today i may be free
you see it as a may
be as it weighs on shoulders
i won't showcase how it feels

but i'm slipping away
trying to hold on to you like murphy
she and i told you to stay
but the look over shoulder wasn't enough
for our future plays
her father yearned for more and yet
he still left to go save the race
you told me it was best
to hit pause and put us at rest
but why as i screamed inside
the back of my head understood
let him go as you should
we both don't deserve what's going on

i still wanna hold you in my arms
night and day as it may
my fluorescent moon
you look to me as you shine the way

the night we met

do you actually want to know me?
take interest in passions none have seen?
brave enough to pick and pull apart whatever's
left of the brain i've so freely promoted
you'll clearly see the ones who've left marks
teared their claws into my walls
you'll see repair-mans in there
each patching year old wounds
from childhood to the twenty first
many to count, none of which
you want to experience
do you like what you see?
am i still interesting enough to you where i seem
familiar and new
maybe my display has tricked you into believing
im flashing green lit good
god i hope my update comes in soon
so you don't have to put up with the repairman's
hand me down conclusion

star treatment

oil paint or telescopic view
black patchy foundation centring tons
beaming flecks illuminate the canvas with
something new,
fantasies etched between mountains of
constellations
i study closely at the evidence you've stranded
before me, i find myself captured by grace
translation of our future visions is aided
giving direct signals to our meeting place
portraying Theodore Finch is a lousy way of
saying goodbye,
but you always liked a good game of hare and
hounds
give it a rest, expecting me to follow and comply
however, it seems that wherever you go, i'll be
around
oh dear, make it last
because you know it all goes so fast

winter's play

i feel all of it sink in
little by little
cars hitting me like speed dial
there's no end
wait there's the finish line
have i gone completely blind
turmoil running through its course
of river lies and sorrow
strobe lights shoot my vision
clear this up right now
this isn't happening
i'm not here, i'm not him
cautionary tale of regret

it seems every where i go
i see the yellow and green hat
guitar on bed, head and back
i cant shake the thought of you
it creeps into my visionary view
and i can feel it orbiting
the sick bit is i'm still needy
even though i feel your knife
for the fifth time in a row
my mind mistakes it for your helping hand
and my wounds declare love
from the bottom of my heart

and see i thought i had come to know you
i told my mom and friends
excited to get closer to you
but to my surprise and demise
or shall i say the opposite truth
i've already seen this story
i know who the twisted one is here
i envy to push away
but my heart wants to play again
the game that gave me the sick
the sick love that i've come to know since
december sixth

help?

do you ever feel like you're sinking?
somethings suffocating me, i can feel it
the grips getting tighter and heavier
one more push and i think i might spiral
race car thoughts are all i have now
they keep pushing through the tracks of my
crowded view
endless moving, no stopping
there's this notion that if i were to stop for even
one second
catch my breath and let a single coherent
feeling slip into my thought process
the constant motion of stained memories
come flooding back, where resent and agony
play tug of war
and the winning prize of this foolish broken
heart is having to deal with all this hurt;
this pain, we can't see it or touch it
a stubborn parasite on the inside of this hollow
frame
i pray to never feel like this again
the start of a never ending curse
how do i continue without crashing
as i ask others for help

mental quotes

i've been resisting the coming apart thoughts
the ones that come at me like comets
slow and burning
the house that's falling apart
i can feel it nearing and close by
almost like it's going to hit me
i don't know what to do
if im stupid or curious
i dread to know if the answer is true
of whether or not you care for me too?

should i plan for disaster?
maybe you can give me a clue
as all the signals point to something new
i doubt you can read my mind
but i can see through you
your body says you want me
but your eyes say not too soon
minds still stuck in the year '22
i kinda would've thought you weren't like the
others
bored, pitiful, but fun and cute

and as i stray to wonder
if you'll ever feel this way

as i lay it on your lips
rage on fingertips
hands squeezing so hard
they recognize the rhythm
of what once was dear
now they can't tell it apart
it feels like he has one foot out the door
and the other stomping on my heart

on repeat

replay on sheffield
you and me dancing
sounds like a match
waiting to catch on fire
it's aching to burn alive
i'm on a live wire
don't touch me
foul spark might ignite the unexpected
touch me
maybe we'll blow a fuse or two
but what if it all fades or explodes
too soon, now i'm back on the road
waiting to find a home
that's yearning for me
my thoughts at ease
is it too early to release
any form of intimacy
that craves comfort and silence
from chest to back
i'm at a disadvantage
wondering how the hell did i get here
it only took a couple of smiles
and i'm already at 4 miles